Brocksport USA

The Maynard Junebug Series

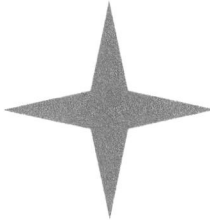

Brocksport USA The Maynard Junebug Series

© Copyright 2012

This is the first in a series about Brocksport and the folks who reside there. Hope you enjoy!

Janice Ernest

Acknowledgements

My thanks to Nikki Brown, a friend who suggested I pursue this group of characters and who has listened to all my ideas with patience. She has been a great encourager of my decision to write this series of stories and to Sharon Ellsberry who saw the potential in Maynard Junebug, Deputy of the Brocksport Police.

Also, my mother who read the stories and then patiently listened to me read them aloud, and still laughed. If it makes a mother happy, it must be good!

To the many other members of the East Texas Writer's Guild without whose support I would never have endeavored to share these stories. www.etwritersguild.org.

And last, but not least, kudos to the Writing Warriors Critique Group: Bobbie Shafer, Pat La Vigne, Linda Nelson Ellis, and Brinda Carey. They have listened, read and made excellent suggestions each step of my writing career.

Table of Contents

Welcome to Brocksport

Welcome to Brocksport. Our fine city is located on the beautiful shores of Lake Cavenclaw. People have even sighted Bigfoot here. (Well, at least they found prints. We're all convinced those big old bare feet belong to Jake Waterville.) He's kind of a backwoods hermit sort that lives close by. Word is he lives in the woods back by Beaver's back strap, at the end of Cavenclaw. We don't recommend you tourists go there.

Well, enough about him. We're the dumpling capital of the world, probably because of a Dutch explorer, Willem Schylenger. He came here a century ago and brought the secret recipe--- at least that's what my mother told me. Every year we celebrate the Spring Dumpling Festival and name a new Ms. Stuffing. Last years was Melody Maltball. She's a real cutie.

Not a lot happens in Brocksport, just the usual stuff. A mailbox vandalized, somebody's underpants were stolen from the clothes line and found hanging from the flag pole out in front of the Do-good elementary school. Took us twenty-five minutes to get those granny pants down. You should have seen Mrs. Della when she ran up and grabbed 'em. That's the fastest any of us have ever seen her move. She looked like Jell-O on legs.

We have all the amenities: A Piggly Wiggly grocery store, a diner owned and operated by the fine Della Dixon. Why, we even have a post office and a police station, along with two police to boot, and we're growing all the time.

So are you planning on staying long? We got some real good camp sites just the other side of town or you could stay at the Baxter's Beggar's Inn. It's a real nice Victorian place down at the end of the street there.

In the meantime, grab a piece of that fresh- from- the- oven apple pie. Set yourself down in that chair right there and I'll fill you in on the people and stories of Brocksport.

What's in the Bag?

Brocksport Police Officer Maynard Junebug's

Nightshift Adventure

What's in the Bag?

Officer Maynard Junebug had driven this country highway a million times, stopping kids speeding in their daddy's' pickup, and pursuing them as they threw beer cans out the window. Why, he even caught a couple of boys with real drugs; two joints to be exact.

He mentally hitched up his drawers and pulled on his imaginary suspenders. *Yes sir ree. The night shift is the best; none of that pansy day shift stuff for me like watching down by the local stop sign or catching jay walkers. Nope, I'm a creature of the night; a vigilant watchdog for all that is good and innocent. But wait....what was that?*

A woman walked along the highway, raven hair pulled up in a tight bun, heart-shaped face, dressed in a peasant blouse and tiered skirt. The moonlight glinted off her hair, gold chain necklace and flowy sequin decorated outfit. Her feet were bare and she glided along the road's edge with the grace of a cat. Gripped in her right hand, a brown paper sack.

"I better check this out." Maynard u-turned.

"Ma'am? Are you all right? What are you doing out here so late at night with no shoes on?" The woman quickened her pace.

Maynard pulled the car over onto the shoulder and spoke into his radio."Officer in pursuit of a lone female who is walking along side of the road while carrying a brown paper sack."

He jumped from the car and started after her. "Ma'am, stop. I need to speak with you.I'm Officer Maynard Junebug of the Brocksport Police." She slowed her pace; he caught up. "Ma'am, are you okay? Did your car break down? And Ma'am what's in the bag?"

She turned to face him; the lines formed by her tears glinted in the brilliant moonlight. The only sound her soft sobs. He touched her arm.

"Ma'am, what's in the bag? Are you lost?"

She wiped her face with her hand then sniffled. "No, I'm going home from the cemetery."

Okay, maybe she is some kind of weirdo witch or gypsy, or something. "Ma'am what's in the bag?"

She handed over the bag; he unfolded it and, as she watched, looked in. Inside was a pair of ballet slippers. "Are these yours Ma'am?"

"Tonight is the anniversary of my daughter, Tonia's death. I had promised her before she died that we would dance together at the full moon. I didn't want to break my promise, so we danced tonight." The tears running down her face glistened like jewels in the moonlight and tugged on Officer Junebug's heartstrings.

"Now, I am on my way home. I live in the next house down." She pointed.

Acknowledging her need to be alone, Maynard went to his car and slowly drove away. He later swore that he could see a sprite-like child, all gossamer, transparent, dancing along behind the woman.

Another night; another story from the night shift. After all, he was Maynard Junebug, Deputy Sheriff of the Brocksport Police. He smiled. *He was a creature of the night-- the vigilant watchdog of all that was good and innocent.*

Paul Mason Is Missing.

Paul Mason is Missing

Everybody in town knew Paul Mason. He was that guy who rode a bicycle with a basket and picked garbage out of trash receptacles. At one time, he was the town banker, had a wife and family and everything until he embezzled $200.00 from the Piggly Wiggly's bank account, that is.

Gossip was that if he had just stolen from someone else he'd still be in business today, but, stealing from a big business like the Piggly Wiggly? Well, that got him jail time, a lost family, a lost home, and a drinking problem. All of us in town liked him. He was kind of like the town mascot. Every day you'd see him pedaling around. Most everyone would say "Hi, Paul" and he would grin that big goofy smile of his back at you, until last Thursday when he suddenly disappeared.

His bicycle was found down by the old mill pond next to the cemetery. Some of us thought he might have drowned himself.

There was talk of dredging the pond, but Reverend Max Tudor stated he'd do a walk-through of it in his baptismal waders since the pond was only waist deep at its deepest.

The whole town came out to watch. Della Dixon even closed down the café and Sheriff Longhorn called in Deputy Junebug.

Grey clouds, pregnant with rain, loomed overhead in the October sky. Everybody stood in reverent wonder at the search that was about to begin. Reverend Tudor quieted the crowd by raising his hand, and staring at them each in turn. Silence filled the moment interrupted only by distant thunder.

"Oh Lord," Rev. Tudor's voice boomed and seemed to communicate with the clouds overhead. "We are gathered here at the pond today to search for our dear neighbor, Paul Mason. Lord, he was a good man, although one in need of saving, but no man deserves to be lost as he has been lost. Go with me as I enter into the abyss of the old mill pond. Amen."

He tightened the suspenders on his black rubber waders so that the top reached his chest making him resemble a big round black tadpole. Toddling to the edge of the pond, he looked up toward the heavens in silent reflection. All serious, hands clasped, he stepped off into the cistern.

He slid his feet along the bottom of the reservoir one slow step at a time until his toes touched something.

"Oh, my Jesus!" He bellowed and stumbled backward, awkwardly maintaining his footing. Whatever his foot had hit was large and pushed inward at his touch. "Sh...Sheriff, I need you in here right now!"

Sheriff Mason Longhorn, raced to the police car and retrieved his waders from the back seat, pulled them on and then trudged back to the pond.

"Junebug, get these people back until we know what we've got here." Sheriff Longhorn waded in next to Reverend Tudor.

Officer Junebug stuck out his sunken chest, strode to the front of the crowd, turned and faced them. Standing with his feet apart, hands on his hips, he reached up and ran his hand along the bill of his police hat to straighten it. "Okay everybody, step back you all, give 'em some room." He marched back and forth in front of the crowd like a pit-bull in a fight circle. *Get close to the 'bug' and you are gonna get bit.*

As the crowd strained to see, Sheriff Longhorn and Rev. Tudor struggled and tugged on the underwater bundle, pulling it toward the bank. A collective gasp was heard as they dragged the man-sized garbage bag enclosed package onto the shore. A cacophony of observations filled the air.

"It's Paul!"

"How horrible!"

"Nothing like this has ever happened before in Brocksport!"

"Oh, my!"

Comments ascended from the crowd like helium balloons and floated on the wind.

"Oh Paul," Della Dixon howled and wrung her hands. She fed him every day at the Dixie Diner, a free meal.

"Oh, Paul." She howled again, her voice traveling like a cheerleader with a bullhorn.

All eyes were on the sopping wet trash bag and the knife with which it was about to be slit open. No one even heard the faint cry from the cemetery.

"I'm over here. Was someone calling me? Hello?"

Paul Mason had been awakened by the howls and groans of the townspeople and especially Della

"Della, is that you?" He rubbed his eyes and looked around at his surroundings. "Huh," he was in some kind of hole." I must have fallen in here last night."

At least it was the most comfortable place he had slept in a long time. The dirt walls and floor of broken up earth served well to keep out the elements and provide a soft mattress.

"No wonder I slept so well. Well, I better get up then."

He scrabbled in the narrow pit and managed to stand up only to discover that the hole was at least six feet deep. He was five foot eight. He jumped and caught on to the sides but then slid back into the hole.

"Oh well, someone will come along and find me, sooner or later." And with that he settled back into his hidey hole for another nap.

Meanwhile at the pond the bag made a 'shunk' noise as the knife slit down its side. Water poured everywhere.

"Oh Dear Lord!" Rev. Tudor slapped his hands to his cheeks as all saw what was in the bag. Sheets wrapped up, tangled, around a bulky body length bundle.

"Junebug, get these people out of here, now." sheriff Longhorn called from the pond's edge.

"You heard him, folks, go back to your homes and businesses now. There's nothing more here for you to see, just some old sheets, that's all. Somebody's laundry."

He began to make shooing motions with his hands and advanced toward the crowd. Reluctantly everyone backed up.

"You will tell me what you found? Won't you? There'll be a piece of homemade apple pie waiting for you at the Diner." Della's eyebrows pinched together as she wrung her hands on her apron.

"Yeah, yeah, Della. I'll let you know." He watched her plump rear-end as she walked to her car. Her buttocks were moving, *No, you go first, no you go first*. Something about that woman really heated his blood. He placed his thumbs in his pockets and sauntered back down to the pond.

"What you got boys?"

Sheriff Longhorn remained head down with a stick in hand probing the soggy pile of debris."Just a bunch of left over stuff from some garage sale somewhere. Some sheets, clothes, kitchen items, that's all." He put down the stick and shook hands with the Reverend.

"Thanks Reverend for your help. I guess I'll get this cleaned up and then head on back to the police station. It's about time for Deputy Junebug to take over for the night. Hey, Junebug, you ready to go?"

"Yes sir." He practically saluted Sheriff Longhorn. "I guess this is one mystery that will go unsolved for now."

Deputy Maynard helped clean up the mess then he and Sheriff Longhorn got in the car and headed for the small square building on Hunter Hayes Street that served as the police station and jail.

"Maynard, it's about time for me to get on home to Maggie May. She's frying up some chicken tonight, so the station and the car are yours. See ya in the morning."

"Yes sir." Maynard Junebug stood still and tried not to fidget with impatience at the slow departure of his boss. As the door to the small police station closed and he heard the Sheriff's car start, he pulled himself up to his full height of five feet eleven inches, took a deep breath, and let it out.

"It's my turn now." He patted his hip where the .38 caliber revolver hung loosely in its holster.
He only carried one bullet which he kept in his pocket in case he should need it. Ever since the time he shot his foot by accident when trying to scare a pesky raccoon out from under Mrs. Smith's house he had decided to keep the chamber of his .38 empty. He could always load that bullet should he need it. He puffed out his chest, bit his lip in determination, and nodded, "Yeah". *After all, I am Maynard Junebug, defender of all that is right and innocent.*

He hooked the jail key ring onto his belt and started out the door. *There is a mystery to be solved in this town and I'm going to solve it, even if it is the last thing I ever do.* "I'll find Paul Mason."

First stop: the old Mill Pond for a quick look around with his flashlight. He pulled the car up to the cemetery gate adjacent to the pond and then got out. The night was dark and crisp.Frogs and bugs were singing in harmony in a nighttime symphony. A breeze blew and the dried autumn leaves crackled on the trees and fell like snowflakes. He stepped cautiously into the circle of light dealt him by his flashlight.

He circled the small pond, shining his light along the way through the reeds and long grass. "Well, no evidence here. I guess I ought to check the cemetery too."

The cemetery gate squealed like a terrified woman. The hair on Maynard's neck stood on end. Shadows played along the tombstones as he showed his light around. *Was that something? Was that someone sitting over there on top of Old Tim's tombstone?*

"Oh Maynard, there's no such thing as ghosts, and if there is, they can't hurt you. They're just a bunch of mist, that's all."

He hitched up his pants and maintained his light on the apparition ahead of him as he forged on.

"Officer Junebug here of the Brocksport Police. I advise you to step away from the tombstone and come to me with your hands in the air." He continued forward.

"Ohhhhh.....oooooooomm!" a deep guttural moan tossed itself over the breeze in a wave.

Maynard Junebug's bladder contracted ready to empty itself. The hair on his arms and neck stood to attention. His heart raced faster than a winning horse in the Kentucky Derby. *Calm yourself, whoa, boy. It's just some kids.*

"Real funny."

He edged forward, his hand now on his weapon. The .38 felt cold to his touch. His flashlight was shaking.

Putting the flashlight in his mouth, he reached up and fumbled in his shirt pocket and found the bullet. "There you are," he muttered as he plucked the ammo from its home. After a struggle, he extricated Bessie, his .38 from her holster. Using his free hand, he tried to open the cylinder on his gun and immediately lost the bullet on the ground in his fumble to load the weapon.

"Great Maynard, just great." He mumbled around the flashlight. He pushed the empty chamber back into his weapon then replaced it in the holster and retrieved the flashlight.

"Lot of good that'll do me. I'll just have to depend on my martial arts skills then." With flashlight in hand, he struck a pose.

"Hi-Ya!" Feeling satisfied he hollered with as much authority as he could muster.

"I told you to come over here, right now with your hands up."

"Ohhh….who's there? I'm over here. Come here."

"Smart guy, eh." He inhaled deeply through his nose, then exhaled and steeled himself for what was to come.

"Well, I'll just come to you." Officer Maynard, his feet leaden, forced himself to step, one, two, three steps. Never taking the light beam off the shadow above the tombstone. Closer, closer to his target; suddenly he was falling, falling. The flashlight fell with him exposing the sides of the hole, all dirt. A freshly dug grave. He landed with a thud on something soft.

The something soft, moaned. "Ow, ohhh. Maynard? Hey, it's me, Paul. You know we're never getting out…"

Maynard flailed about blindly, dropping his flashlight Before Paul's sentence was completed Junebug jumped atop Paul using him as a springboard and jumped out of the hole, and then took off at a run.

"Ow, that hurt. Hey, come back! Don't leave me here!" Paul shined the flashlight over the edge of the hole.

Maynard had almost reached the car when he heard Paul's voice wafting on the breeze.

"Maynard, come get me out of this hole, right now. Do you hear me? I haven't eaten all day and I need a drink."

Get a grip Maynard. Go back to the hole; get your flashlight, after all, a ghost can't hurt you. He hitched up his drawers and headed back to the cemetery where he found Paul sitting cross-legged in the hole.

"Hey, Maynard help me out of here."

"No problem." Maynard got on his knees and offered Paul a hand up.

"Maynard?"

"Yeah."

"Did I scare you?"

"Are you kidding? Of course not. I knew it was you in there the whole time, I just had to go back to the car and call in that I found ya, that's all."

"Oh, okay. Can you drop me off at Dixie's place? I sure am hungry. I can pick up my bike tomorrow."

He tilted his head in assent. "You bet I can."

Another case solved by Maynard Junebug, defender of the weak. Smarter than the average guy. Hero to the homeless. Fearless. That's me all right, Officer Maynard Junebug of the Brocksport Police.

Some En-<u>Bat</u>tled Evening

Some En-Battled Evening

Betty and John Baxter had just settled in for the night; she in her full-length nightgown with the ruffled neck, and he in his flannel pajama pants and shirt. They were cozy as two bears snuggled together during winter hibernation.

Moonlight streamed in through the open window. John always liked it open this time of year, said it made the room fresh and cool. Sleeping was just somehow better in the crisp, cold night air.

If he could have, he would have been born a wolf, roaming the night, howling till dawn, but alas, he was only a man.

Sounds of the night filled the room. Night creatures tuned their voices: crickets rubbed their legs together; locusts and June bugs buzzed; frogs croaked; the symphony of the dark had begun. A lone owl hooted in the oak tree over at Dean Johnson's house. Bats chirped and sent out sound feelers for a tasty morsel.

John snored like a freight train, adding his part to the melody and Betty lightly joined in with her gentle respirations. The moon smiled in through the window. All was well in Brocksport, tonight. For everyone…except a confused bat, that is.

The wayward bat flew through the open window into Betty and John's bedroom and in desperation, sent out sonar chirps trying to find his way back out into the open night sky.

His problem: The sounds were reverberating off the walls all around him making it virtually impossible to find his exit.

He bumped into walls and flew to the ceiling and hung from the ceiling fan, trying to get his bearings.
Then he would take flight again.

He ran haphazard into the light on Betty's side of the bed. The lamp went flying off the table awakening Betty.

In desperation, the bat flew down and brushed Betty, who screamed and shoved John hard, waking him in mid snore.

"Wha…? What's going on?" He rubbed his eyes with his fists. "What'd you do that for?"

Betty, now hidden under the covers, cried out. "Bat! Bat!"

"Bat? What are you talking about? What do you mean 'bat'?"

At that same moment, the bat who was yelling "Humans! Humans!" in bat language, tried once more to fly out.

This time, as John was trying to sit up in the bed the poor beast hit him head on stunning both bat and human for a few seconds.

"Oh my God, Batty, it's a bet! No, I mean bat!"
Her muffled voice through the sheet responded.

"Yes, there's a bat in here. You've got to take care of it, John, right now!"

Roaches and spiders I can handle, but wrangle a bat?

"Betty get the phone and dial 911? I'll try to do something with the bat, but if he bites me, they carry rabies you know." He jumped from the bed and made a flying leap for the door.

A hand reached out from under the covers on Betty's side of the bed, groped for the cell phone, grabbed it, then like 'thing' in the Adams Family shows of old, disappeared under the sheet. An eerie glow could be seen as the cell phone came to life at Betty's touch.

"Help! Police! There's a bet in our batroom…No, a bat…No, not a man with a bat, a bat, you know fangs, a creature of the night, flies around, hangs upside down…yes, that kind of bat. It's in our bedroom. My husband is trying to get it right now. Can you send someone? Please? My husband is a heart patient you know. Yes, we're at 42 Lillian Boulevard. Hurry, please."

The light flickered off. "Honey, I called the police, Maynard should be here soon."

"Honey?" The room was silent without response.

"Honey?" She pulled down the sheet in time to see him entering the room. Dressed in his padded ski jacket and ski pants, and wearing a pillowcase on his head with two holes for his eyes, entered John Baxter. On his left hand, he wore an oven mitt and in that oven-mitted hand he was holding a tennis racket.

In his right hand, he carried a thirty gallon Rubbermaid trash can with a lid. He trundled over to Betty's side of the bed and set the trash can down, then removed the lid to use as a shield in his right hand.

"John, what are you doing?" she said from her safe haven enshrouded in sheets.

"Getting the bat." He grumbled and proceeded to climb up on the bed and swat at the bat with the tennis racket. Unable to see well through his two eye holes, he flailed around aimlessly at the air looking like some kind of alien doing a rain dance.

The bat, curious about this change of events, left his perch and flew slowly around John, trying to see what form of creature he was dealing with.

The closer the bat flew, the more exaggerated and crazy John's dance became. Finally, he fell over Betty and into the trashcan headfirst, where he lay pinned, head, shoulders, and upper arms in the trash can and motionless.

"John? John?" Betty peered out from beneath her covers. The moonlight streamed through the window outlining John's silhouette on the floor. Jammed in the trash can he lay wedged between the bed and the open window, bent at the waist, his legs sticking up above Betty's side of the bed. She grabbed onto his foot.

"Oh God, John? John?"

"Yeah," his muffled angry voice responded.

"Did you get the bat?"

"No."

The sound of a lone police siren filled the air growing louder as Maynard Junebug, Deputy of the Brocksport Police approached.

Finally a real call in the night. They said it was a bat, maybe it was a burglar. His heart beat faster than a hummingbird as he exited the car. He checked out the house...upstairs window open, lights off.

"Yep, could be a burglar with a bat. I need to be prepared for anything."

He checked to make sure his .38 was in its holster, practiced a quick draw one time. "Okay, buddy put down the bat or I'll have to shoot ya."

Yep, that's how I'll handle it. Cool, calm, and collected, that's me. He loaded his lone bullet into the .38 and closed the chamber.

"Bessie, don't let me down tonight." He holstered the gun and patted it lovingly.

"Yep, this is the real thing all right." He took a deep breath through his nose, ambled to the front door and knocked.

No answer, then he heard Betty's voice from the upstairs window.

"Maynard, we're up here."

"How do I get in?" He looked around for a way in.

"Use the key under the ceramic turtle on the porch there." He reached down and sure enough under the ceramic turtle was the key to the front door.He checked his gun one more time.

"Everything all right in there?"

"Yes. Maynard just get the key and come on. We need your help up here." The response was muffled and foot tapping angry.

He cautiously opened the door. Having never been in a situation quite like this one he had to rely on his knowledge of TV shows like "Law and Order". You never know what might be waiting inside.

He entered and slammed himself up against the wall, pulling his gun and pointing it ahead of him. Not seeing trouble he slid with his back against the wall all the way to the stairs where he turned all around, gun in hand, ready for danger. All clear. He headed up the stairs.

"Hurry up, Maynard, I've fallen and I can't get up." John was lying on his back, with the many layers of clothing and the garbage can over his head pinning his arms he was unable to move.

Maynard raced toward the sound of his voice. "I'm coming."

Maynard reached the open bedroom door. *Okay, Maynard old man, get ready.*

He leaped around the corner into the bedroom, feet apart, weapon in hand. His head swiveled from side to side looking for any sign of danger.

Betty, who was peeking out from beneath the covers, screamed so loud that lights went on in the houses on both sides of hers.

Maynard shouted and pulled the trigger. The single bullet shot a hole right through the wall over Betty's side of the bed.

"Maynard, you almost killed me? Are you out of your mind?" Betty peered at him. Her brown eyes glistened in the moonlight.

"Oh Lord, Mrs. Betty, you scared the bejesus out of me. Now, what's going on?" He lowered the weapon.

"B-B-B-Bat!" Betty pointed at the ceiling fan where the now exhausted bat hung upside down.

"Well, aren't you cute?" Maynard went up to the bat and looked it right in its beady little eyes.

"You're a little bit lost, aren't you fella? Well, I can help you out. Got your sonar all screwed up in here in this enclosed space."

"Mrs. Betty you just stay put and Mr. John don't you move. I'll get this little guy out of here in no time."

Maynard walked to the window and began to make small chirping noises and clicking sounds. The bat turned its head toward the sounds, then after a few seconds took off and out the window.

"Hey Maynard," a muffled voice came from under the garbage can. "Can you help me out here?"

"Why sure." Maynard bent down and extricated Mr. Baxter from the trash can, and then helped him sit up straight.

"Maynard?" Mrs. Betty peeked out from her covers. "Is the bat gone now?"

"Yes ma'am he just needed a little traffic direction. Y'all will be just fine now. Is there anything else I can do for ya?" He placed his hands on his waist, feet apart, and took in a deep nasal inhale.

"No, but thank you so much. "

Maynard made his exit, still wondering why Mr. Baxter was wearing a pillowcase over his head with two eye holes, an oven mitten, and a ski suit. His job was not to wonder about their private behaviors; his job was simply to defend the innocent and bring criminals to justice, even if the criminal was a bat in the night.

He got into the police car, turned on the engine, and smiled to himself. *Yep, another story from the night shift.*

About the Author

Born in East Texas, Janice Ernest spent her school years in Houston and couldn't wait to get back to the country. So, in the 1970's she left the big city and headed to a smaller, sophisticated city near Dallas, Texas and has been there ever since. She now lives in East Texas with her mother and two dogs, Patsy Marie, and Pearl May.

She is a member of the East Texas Writer's Guild, and a past member of The East Texas Writer's Association, and the North East Texas Writer's Organization and would love to visit with you or speak to your group. You may contact Janice at:

http://www.janiceernest.com

janiceernest1@gmail.com

Or join me on Facebook at Janice Ernest, Author

Turn the page to see more short books and novels by this author

Need More Brocksport?

Check out the rest of the **Brocksport series—Brocksport: Back Again?** Come back for a second helping of Brocksport. This book tells the story of Delton Sr. and Lucy LaMour, and Delton Jr. and his new wife, Moonbeam LaMour. You'll see the regular group of characters: Paul Mason, Della Dixon, Mason Longhorn, and our friend Deputy Officer Maynard Junebug. You'll also meet a turkey named Lewis, and learn more about Jake Waterville mentioned in the first book. Look forward to fun and high jinks in this new installment. Check out my website www.janiceernest.com, click on the Brocksport USA page and sign up to be a citizen of Brocksport. Hope to see you there.

Make sure and keep your eyes open for the third in the series: **Brocksport: It Couldn't Happen Here!** This one should be out by December of 2015. Join Della Dixon and Maynard Junebug as they seek to solve a mystery and keep a crime from occuring.

More shorts and books by Janice Ernest:

Bye, Bye Sweet Sammy—Macy Starks has caught her husband cheating. How will she handle it? Hell hath no fury like a woman scorned. (Short but an excellent read)

The Glider—A short story about a man whose wife has died. He sits on the glider on his porch and remembers different times in their life together. It shows how life is a cycle, love, birth, growth, and death and it all starts over again. After you read this one, go to my website www.janiceernest.com and download a "Let's Make a Memory" certificate to give to a loved one.(There are items of a sexual nature in this book.)

Butterfly—A full-length novel. Anna Marie Minguez goes out on the town unchaperoned for the first time in New Orleans at Mardi Gras. She meets a man, gets raped, and becomes his captive.

Her faith in God and the people he puts in her path help her to make it through. Her love for her captor; can it change his heart? Could he love her too? Could he change for her? (there are items of graphic sexual nature in this book.)

To be followed by **<u>Taking Flight</u>**, Cozette Gauvain suffered abuse in the past which has caused her to feel she is worthless. So worthless, that she lives wrecklessly. Impregnated by Gangster, Bobby McDamion, she seeks a way to legitamize herself and obtain financial security for her newborn. MaxMonteaux, a crooked attorney, offers her partnership if she plays a part in his scheme. Is her life worthy of true love and respect? Or will she be thrust aside once again?

If you enjoyed Brocksport, USA please feel free to write a review and share with your friends. Reviews can be posted on Amazon.com, Kindle, Goodreads.com. or on your Facebook. Get Brocksportian and help Brocksport grow.